Playing Presents

Shakespeare's

Two Gentlemen of Verona

FOR KIDS
(The melodramatic version!)

For 5-16+ actors, or kids of all ages who want to have fun!
Creatively modified by
Suzy Newman and Brendan P. Kelso
Cover layout by Shana Hallmeyer
Cover characters by Ron Leishman
Special Contributor: Asif Zamir

3 Melodramatic Modifications of Shakespeare's Play
for 3 different group sizes:

5-8 actors

7-10 actors

10-16+ actors

Table Of Contents

To all of those who pursue art, on the stage, page, playground or living room. And to all those who support art, with their time, talent, money or encouragement.

-Suzy

To Two Gentlemen of SLO (cough, cough...)
Steve & Rodney C.
Thank you for opening my eyes and believing in my entrepreneurial spirit!

-BPK

For performance rights please see page 6 of this book or contact:

contact@PlayingWithPlays.com

Foreword

When I was in high school there was something about Shakespeare that appealed to me. Not that I understood it mind you, but there were clear scenes and images that always stood out in my mind. Romeo & Juliet, "Romeo, Romeo; wherefore art thou Romeo?"; Julius Caesar, "Et tu Brute"; Macbeth, "Double, Double, toil and trouble"; Hamlet, "to be or not to be"; A Midsummer Night's Dream, all I remember about this was a wickedly cool fairy and something about a guy turning into a donkey that I thought was pretty funny. It was not until I started analyzing Shakespeare's plays as an actor that I realized one very important thing, I still didn't understand them. Seriously though, it's tough enough for adults, let alone kids. Then it hit me, why don't I make a version that kids could perform, but make it easy for them to understand with a splash of Shakespeare lingo mixed in? And voila! A melodramatic masterpiece was created! They are intended to be melodramatically fun!

THE PLAYS: There are 3 plays within this book, for three different group sizes. The reason: to allow educators or parents to get the story across to their children regardless of the size of their group. As you read through the plays, there are several lines that are highlighted. These are actual lines from the original book. I am a little more particular about the kids saying these lines verbatim. But the rest, well... have fun!

The entire purpose of this book is to instill the love of a classic story, as well as drama, into the kids.

And when you have children who have a passion for something, they will start to teach themselves, with or without school.

These plays are intended for pure fun. Please DO NOT have the kids learn these lines verbatim, that would be a complete waste of creativity. But do have them basically know their lines and improvise wherever they want as long as it pertains to telling the story. Because that is the goal of an actor: to tell the story. In A Midsummer Night's Dream, I once had a student playing Quince question me about one of her lines, "but in the actual story, didn't the Mechanicals state that 'they would hang us'?" I thought for a second and realized that she had read the story with her mom, and she was right. So I let her add the line she wanted and it added that much more fun, it made the play theirs. I have had kids throw water on the audience, run around the audience, sit in the audience, lose their pumpkin pants (size 30 around a size 15 doesn't work very well, but makes for some great humor!) and most importantly, die all over the stage. The kids love it.

One last note: if you want some educational resources, loved our plays, want to tell the world how much your kids loved performing Shakespeare, want to insult someone with our Shakespeare Insult Generator, or are just a fan of Shakespeare, then hop on our website and have fun:

PlayingWithPlays.com

With these notes, I'll see you on the stage, have fun, and break a leg!

SCHOOL, AFTERSCHOOL, and SUMMER classes

I've been teaching these plays as afterschool and summer programs for quite some time. Many people have asked what the program is, therefore, I have put together a basic formula so any teacher or parent can follow and have melodramatic success! As well, many teachers use my books in a variety of ways. You can view the formula and many more resources on my website at: PlayingWithPlays.com

- Brendan

OTHER PLAYS AND FULL LENGTH SCRIPTS

We have over 25 different titles, as well as a full-length play in 4-acts for theatre groups: Shakespeare's Hilarious Tragedies. You can see all of our other titles on our website here: PlayingWithPlays.com/books

As well, you can see a sneak peek at some of those titles at the back of this book.

And, if you ever have any questions, please don't hesitate to ask at: Contact@PlayingWithPlays.com

ROYALTIES

If you have any questions about royalties or performance licenses, here are the basic guidelines:

1) Please contact us! We always LOVE to hear about a school or group performing our books! We would also love to share photos and brag about your program as well! (with your permission, of course)

2) If you are a group and DO NOT charge your kids to be in this production, contact us about discounted copyright fees (one way or another, we will make this work for you!) You are NOT required to buy a book per kid (but, we will still send you some really cool Shakespeare tattoos for your kids!)

3) If you are a group and DO charge your kids to be in the production, (i.e. afterschool program, summer camp) we ask that you purchase a book per kid. Contact us as we will give you a bulk discount (10 books or more) and send some really cool press on Shakespeare tattoos!

4) If you are a group and DO NOT charge the audience to see the plays, please see our website FAQs to see if you are eligible to waive the performance royalties (most performances are eligible).

5) If you are a group and DO charge the audience to see the performance, please see our website FAQs for performance licensing fees (this includes performances for donations and competitions).

Any other questions or comments, please see our website or email us at:

contact@PlayingWithPlays.com

The 15-Minute or so
Two Gentlemen of Verona
By William Shakespeare
Creatively modified by
Suzy Newman and Brendan P. Kelso
5-8 Actors

CAST OF CHARACTERS:

VALENTINE: Best buds with Proteus

PROTEUS: Best buds with Valentine and LOVES Julia

JULIA: LOVES Proteus

SILVIA: In love with Valentine

[1]**LUCETTA:** Julia's best friend!

[2]**ANTONIO (ANTONIA):** Proteus' father (mother)

[2]**DUKE (DUCHESS):** Silvia's father (mother)

[1]**SPEED:** Valentine's lackey

The same actors can play the following part:

[1]LUCETTA and SPEED

[2]ANTONIO and DUKE

LUCETTA, SPEED, DUKE, and ANTONIO can all be played by one nimble actor with small costume piece changes.

ACT 1 SCENE 1

(enter VALENTINE and PROTEUS)

PROTEUS: Dude! DUDE! Valentine! Come on. Don't go! You're my best friend!

VALENTINE: Cease to persuade, Proteus! Knock it off! I want to see the wonders of the world abroad! I'm not going to be some dude who lives in his parents' basement and plays video games all day!

PROTEUS: I don't do that! Not all day.

VALENTINE: I know. Most of the time you're talking about Julia. Julia this *(big teasing sigh)*, Julia that *(sigh)*. I would ask you come with me, but I know you'd rather stay here in boring old Verona and think about Julia. Julia, Julia, Julia! *(kiss kiss kissy face to Proteus)*

PROTEUS: Fine! And someday you'll meet someone who you can't stop thinking about. And then you'll, think on thy Proteus! *(points to self)*

VALENTINE: Whatever. Take it easy.

(they secret handshake, fist bump, hug...)

VALENTINE: I'm out! *(exits)*

PROTEUS: *(calling after)* Later, dude! Have fun in Milan! *(pause)* Julia! *(sighs, exactly in the way Valentine mocked him; enter SPEED)*

SPEED: Proteus! Did you see my master?

PROTEUS: Hey, Speed! *(to audience)* Yeah, his name is Speed, don't ask, not like he's actually fast! *(to SPEED)* Yeah, he left two seconds ago, to embark for Milan.

SPEED: Bummer! Twenty to one then he is shipp'd already.

(SPEED starts to go)

PROTEUS: Hey! Wait up! Did you give my note to Julia?

SPEED: Huh? Yeah, I gave it to her.

PROTEUS: What did she say? Did she ask about me?

SPEED: Truly, sir, I think you'll hardly win her.

PROTEUS: Why? How can you tell? What did she do?

SPEED: Like I said, she did nothing. You are meant for each other. *(exit SPEED)*

PROTEUS: Argggg!

(exit PROTEUS)

ACT 1 SCENE 2

(enter JULIA and LUCETTA)

JULIA: OK, Lucetta, now that we're alone, let's talk about boys.

LUCETTA: Again?!

JULIA: Yes! Ok, what do you think of......Eglamour?

LUCETTA: Good dresser, nice hair, boring.

JULIA: What about.... Mercatio?

LUCETTA: Drives a nice car, can't speak in full sentences.

JULIA: What....about.....Proteus?

LUCETTA: WOW!!!

JULIA: He's pretty cute, right?

LUCETTA: SUPER cute.

JULIA: So... would you have me cast my love on him?

LUCETTA: Well, maybe you should peruse this paper.

JULIA: 'To Julia.' Who is it from?

LUCETTA: Valentine's page, and sent, I think, from Proteus.

JULIA: Hang on! You had a note for me this whole time?

LUCETTA: Don't be mad. Read it! Tell me what it says!

JULIA: Go, get you gone! I'll tear it to bits before I let you see what it says.

LUCETTA: No you won't.

JULIA: No? *(tears up the letter and throws the pieces into the air)*

LUCETTA: Rude!

(exit LUCETTA stomping her feet and pouting)

JULIA: *(gathering all the pieces of paper frantically)*

No, no, no, no, no, no! Look! Here's my name! 'kind Julia.' Here's his name...Proteus. And here's the word love. *(Resumes gathering the pieces)* Would've been easier if he'd sent a text!

(exit JULIA)

ACT 1 SCENE 3

(enter PROTEUS)

PROTEUS: Sweet love! Sweet lines! Sweet life! Oooo, poetic! I should write that down! *(to audience)* Look! She wrote me another note! She loves me, I love her. Life is perfect. Except we're afraid to tell our parents.

(enter ANTONIO)

ANTONIO: How now! What letter are you reading there?

PROTEUS: Oh! Hey dad! This letter? Oh, it's nothing.

ANTONIO: It's not nothing.

PROTEUS: Ahhhhh......It's a letter from Valentine, telling me what a great time he's having in Milan, yeah... that's what it says!

ANTONIO: Awesome! Glad to hear it! Because, you leave tomorrow to join Valentine in Milan.

PROTEUS: What!? Dad! No way! I don't want... I mean, I need some time. I've got some things to do.

ANTONIO: Like what?

PROTEUS: You know...things! Important things! And stuff! Lots of stuff!

ANTONIO: No more excuses! Go pack your bag.
(ANTONIO begins to exit)

PROTEUS: Fie!

ANTONIO: What was that?

PROTEUS: Fiiii......ne with me, Pops! *(ANTONIO exits)* I was afraid to show my father Julia's letter, lest he should take exceptions to my love; and my own lie of an excuse made it easier for him to send me away.

ANTONIO: *(offstage)* Proteus! Get a move on!!

PROTEUS: Fie!!!

(ALL exit)

ACT 2 SCENE 1

(enter VALENTINE and SPEED following)

VALENTINE: Ah, Silvia, Silvia! *(heavy sighs)*

SPEED: *(mocking)* Madam Silvia! Madam Silvia! Gag me.

VALENTINE: Knock it off! You don't know her.

SPEED: Do too. She's the one that you can't stop staring at. Makes me wanna barf.

VALENTINE: I do not stare!

SPEED: You do. AND you keep singing that silly love song. *(sing INSERT SAPPY LOVE SONG)* You used to be so much fun.

VALENTINE: Huh? *(heavy sigh, starts humming SAME LOVE SONG)*

SPEED: Never mind.

VALENTINE: I have loved her ever since I saw her. Here she comes!

SPEED: Great. *(to audience)* Watch him turn into a fool.

(enter SILVIA)

VALENTINE: Hey, Silvia.

SILVIA: Hey, Valentine. What's goin' on?

VALENTINE: Nothin'. What's goin' on with you?

SILVIA: Nothin'.

(pause)

VALENTINE: What are you doing later?

SILVIA: Not sure. Prob-ly nothin'. You?

VALENTINE: Me neither. Nothin'.

SILVIA: Yea?

VALENTINE: Probably.

SPEED: *(to audience)* Kill me now.

SILVIA: Well, I guess I better go.

VALENTINE: Oh, okay! See ya'..

(pause)

SILVIA: See ya' later maybe?

VALENTINE: Oh, yea! Maybe! Yea! Okay!

SILVIA: Bye.

VALENTINE: Bye!

(exit SILVIA)

SPEED: *(aside)* Wow. *(to VALENTINE)* Dude, what the heck was that?

VALENTINE: I think she has a boyfriend. I can tell.

SPEED: Dude! She is so into you! How could you not see that?

VALENTINE: Do you think?

SPEED: Come on. We'll talk it through over dinner. *(to audience)* Fool. Am I right?

(ALL exit)

ACT 2 SCENE 2

(enter PROTEUS and JULIA)

PROTEUS: Julia, please don't cry. When possibly I can, I will return.

JULIA: This is so unfair, *(sob)* we JUST found each other 10 minutes ago. Here! Take my ring to remember me.

PROTEUS: Awesome! And I'll give you mine.

(they exchange rings)

JULIA: And seal the bargain with a holy kiss. *(PROTEUS is excited)* But, not in front of my parents! *(points to audience)* Let's high-five!

PROTEUS: Julia, I promise you, I'll be thinking about you, like, aaallllllll the time! *(getting dramatic)* And I will love only you, Julia, forever and forever until the end of time.

JULIA: You promise?

PROTEUS: I promise! *("cross my heart and hope to die" motions)*

JULIA: I promise too!

(exit JULIA melodramatically sobbing)

PROTEUS: Julia, farewell! I am so so SO bummed. I LOVE HER SO MUCH!!!

(exit PROTEUS)

(enter SILVIA, VALENTINE, and SPEED)

SILVIA: *(super flirty)* Hey, Vallie wallentine.

VALENTINE: *(same)* Hey, Princess Silvia wilvia.

SILVIA: Break! Here comes my father! *(they separate)*

(enter DUKE)

DUKE: Hey, Valentine. There's another guy here, from Verona, who wants to work for me and I think you know him. His name is Proteus.

VALENTINE: Awesome! He's my best friend! This is great!

DUKE: Terrific, I'll send him out to say 'hi' before I put him to work.

(exit DUKE)

VALENTINE: This is my friend I told you about! The one who would have come along with me except that he is so in love and didn't want to leave his girlfriend.

SILVIA: Did they break up?

VALENTINE: Oh, no. He said many times he will love her till he dies. Kind of how I feel about a certain snooky-wooky, lovey pie...

(enter PROTEUS; they are oblivious to him; he clears his throat to get their attention)

VALENTINE: Welcome, dear Proteus! Silvia, I want you to meet my best friend in the whole world. Proteus, meet Silvia.

SILVIA: *(shaking his hand)* Any friend of Valentine is a friend of mine.

PROTEUS: *(totally struck by her beauty, not letting go of her hand and acting delirious)* Bleen kack hoofta meep.

SILVIA: You're a crack up! We'll have a great time while you're here.

VALENTINE: No doubt. This is going to be the best.

PROTEUS: Plaaaff tooky ponga poop.

SILVIA: I'll leave you two to catch up.

(exit SILVIA)

VALENTINE: Proteus, fill me in! How does your lady? And how thrives your love?

PROTEUS: Oh, you don't want to hear about her. I know you don't like to talk about love.

VALENTINE: Well, that was before. I get it now! Because, guess what? I'm in love, too!

PROTEUS: With who?

VALENTINE: With Silvia!

PROTEUS: Her? But she loves you?

VALENTINE: Yes! And - don't tell anyone - we're going to run away and get married before her dad decides she has to marry some rich dude she doesn't even like and I can't believe I just blurted out all my plans to you!

PROTEUS: No worries. You know I always keep secrets. Those, and promises.

VALENTINE: And, dude, gotta go, I've been away from Silvia for like, two minutes, so... *(high-fives him)* later, bro!

(exit VALENTINE)

PROTEUS: *(Speaks to audience)* I am so so SO totally in love with Silvia! I know, I know... I said I was in love with... what'shername, but this time it's for real. Ooooo, this could be a problem. *(slowly)* My best friend is in love with the girl I love and the girl I used to love is in love with me and we exchanged promise rings and the girl I love now is in love with my best friend, who suddenly I don't really like that much - I don't know why. And they're eloping tonight! Ooooo I'm telling! *(pauses and looks back at audience)* Did you get all that? You have to love confusing Shakespeare comedy!

(exit PROTEUS)

(enter JULIA and LUCETTA)

JULIA: Lucetta! I have the best idea! But I need your help. I'm going to go to Milan and surprise Proteus!

LUCETTA: Wow! Are you sure that's a good idea?

JULIA: Yes! Now, help me make a disguise. I'm going to dress as a boy so no one will bother me.

LUCETTA: OK!

(ALL exit)

ACT 3 SCENE 1

(enter DUKE and PROTEUS)

DUKE: I heard you wanted to talk to me, Proteus. What's up?

(If one actor is playing the multiple roles, DUKE, can be visibly disheveled, exhausted or come in almost wearing the wrong thing, etc. here; use the reality of the situation for a joke!)

PROTEUS: Ooooo, well....

DUKE: Spit it out.

PROTEUS: SilviareallylovesValentineandValentinelovesherandtonighttthey'regoingtoelope

DUKE: WHAT!?!? I am maaaaaaaad! Oh, looky, here comes Valentine. Make yourself scarce. *(exit PROTEUS; enter VALENTINE)*

DUKE: Say, Valentine, where are you going in such a hurry?

VALENTINE: Nowhere.

DUKE: Really? Because you're going in the direction of my daughter with a suspicious look in your eye.

VALENTINE: Whaaaa? Me? No.

DUKE: Seriously? Then why did I find a ladder outside her window with your name marked on it in Sharpie? Get out! You are banish-ed. Ba-nish-ed! And if I ever see you around here again, I'll..... I'll be really REALLY MAD!

(exit DUKE)

VALENTINE: Why not death rather than living torment? *(to audience)* Wow. I get really poetic when I'm miserable. *(pause)* Don't look at me anymore. I'm probably going to cry.

(enter PROTEUS)

PROTEUS: Valentine! We've been looking for you!

VALENTINE: Proteus, my best friend who would never betray me. You'll never guess what happened!

PROTEUS: I heard, I was listening from backstage. But don't worry, I'll help you!

VALENTINE: You will?! You are SUCH a good friend. How will you help me?

PROTEUS: You've got to go far away.

VALENTINE: Well, I'm not sure how that helps me, but I trust you, so OK.

(ALL exit)

(enter JULIA in boys' clothes)

JULIA: Well, I'm here in Milan. Now to find Proteus. *(JULIA looks off-stage)* Here he comes. I'll surprise him. He'll love it!

(she hides; enter DUKE and PROTEUS)

PROTEUS: You have nothing to worry about. Valentine is gone and I'll go talk to Silvia and tell her that Valentine changed his mind about her. Trust me!

DUKE: Of course I trust you. Why wouldn't I?

(exit DUKE)

PROTEUS: *(to audience)* Yikes! I'm having a hard time keeping all of my lies straight!

JULIA: *(to audience)* There he is! He's going to be so happy to see me!

PROTEUS: *(to audience)* Here comes Silvia! *(to Silvia, in a mushy, dreamy voice)* Hiiiiii!

SILVIA: You again! Stop following me! You know I love Valentine.

PROTEUS: Just give me a chance!

SILVIA: No way! *(exiting)*

PROTEUS: Come on! I totally get you. Valentine doesn't get you the way I get you!

JULIA: Whoa. This is NOT going like I planned.

(PROTEUS sees her)

PROTEUS: You there, boy! What's your name?

JULIA: Um...uh, Sebastian? Yup, Sebastian, that's my name.

PROTEUS: You look familiar.... Anyway, I've got a job for you.

JULIA: Okay?

PROTEUS: See that girl that was just here? Go give her this ring that my girlfriend gave me that I said I'd keep forever. I'll pay you.

JULIA: Alas!

PROTEUS: What? What does that mean, and why did you say it?

JULIA: It's an interjection used as an exclamation to express pity or concern or grief. And I said it for your girlfriend.

PROTEUS: Boy, you're complicated.

JULIA: Because methinks that she loved you as well as you do love your lady Silvia, and now you're being really mean to her.

PROTEUS: Whatever. Give her the ring, then come tell me what she said.

(exit PROTEUS)

JULIA: Great. This is that LAST thing I want to do. *(enter SILVIA)* Are you Silvia?

SILVIA: What if I am?

JULIA: I was sent by Proteus to give you this ring.

SILVIA: No way. That's the ring his girlfriend, Julia, gave him and I'm not touching it. We girls have to stick together. Now excuse me while I run away into a dark and scary forest to find my boyfriend, Valentine. *(exit SILVIA)*

JULIA: *(to audience)* Wow. She's pretty cool.

(exit JULIA)

ACT 4 SCENE 1

(enter VALENTINE)

VALENTINE: Well, I'm still depressed but at least it's quiet and beautiful out here in the forest. *(Offstage ruckus)* Hark! Who comes here? *(hides to watch)*

(enter PROTEUS, SILVIA, and JULIA)

PROTEUS: Madam, this service I have done for you, I saved you from getting lost in this creepy forest.

VALENTINE: *(to audience)* How like a dream is this I see and hear! Love, lend me patience to forbear awhile. *(Valentine hides)*

SILVIA: O miserable, unhappy that I am!

PROTEUS: Nooooo! You WERE unhappy, but now I rescued you so now you ARE happy.

SILVIA: I would've rather been eaten by a lion, than have been rescued by you.

PROTEUS: You are really starting to frustrate me.

JULIA: *(to audience)* How do you think I feel?

SILVIA: Get this through your head, I don't like you! I will never go out with you!

PROTEUS: Oh, yes you will. *(goes in for the kiss; closes his eyes and puckers his lips toward her)*

SILVIA: *(running away, screaming)* Ewwwwww!

VALENTINE: *(jumping out)* Ruffian! You better back off if you know what's good for you!!!

PROTEUS/SILVIA/JULIA: Valentine!

VALENTINE: You are seriously the worst best friend ever!

PROTEUS: *(very over melodramatically)* My shame and guilt confounds me. Forgive me, Valentine. *(laying on the floor at his feet)*

VALENTINE: Well, OK. I forgive you. And you can go out with Silvia if you want.

SILVIA & JULIA: WHAT?!?!?!

SILVIA: Valentine! We need to talk!

PROTEUS: Sebastian! Where's that ring you were supposed to give Silvia?

JULIA: Here 'tis; this is it.

PROTEUS: Why, this is the ring I gave to Julia.

JULIA: Oops! Wrong one. THIS is the ring you sent to Silvia.

PROTEUS: How did you get that other one. That's the one I gave to Julia.

JULIA: Yes, it is. And guess what: Julia has brought it here.

(JULIA removes disguise; EVERYONE gasps)

PROTEUS: Uh, oh. How! Julia!

JULIA: Yes, it's me. The one who promised to be true to you. Boy, I feel like a real fool.

PROTEUS: No, please, don't. I'M the fool.

SILVIA: You got that right.

VALENTINE: How about we all just forget any of this ever happened and we have a double wedding!

PROTEUS: Yes! That's a great idea!

(enter DUKE and, if cast size permits, EVERYONE ELSE with general hubbub)

DUKE: What's happened? Is everyone OK? Where's my daughter?

VALENTINE: She's here. Safe and sound. I love her and she loves me and we'd like to get married.

DUKE: If this is what makes Silvia happy, I will consent to this marriage.

VALENTINE: I love happy endings! Come on everyone, let's go prepare for the weddings!

(ALL start rejoicing, except JULIA and SILVIA)

JULIA: HOLD IT! I know Shakespeare says I'm supposed to agree with this and we all live happily ever after, but... no way! I deserve better than someone who forgets me the second I'm out of sight.

SILVIA: You said it, sister!

JULIA: Proteus, here's your ring back. I'm going home.

(exit JULIA)

PROTEUS: *(exits chasing JULIA)* But, Julia, wait... let's talk about it!

SILVIA: Valentine, let's go plan our wedding!

(VALENTINE and SILVIA exit)

DUKE: Well this is awkward. Someone give me a script.

(script is handed to DUKE who looks through)

DUKE: Let's see... Here we go:

"Come, let us go, we will include all jars

With triumphs, mirth, and rare solemnity."

I'm not sure I understand all of that, but it's my line and it sounds like a happy ending to me. Let's go party!!!

(exit DUKE whooping it up)

THE END

NOTES

The 20-Minute or so Two Gentlemen of Verona
By William Shakespeare
Creatively modified by
Brendan P. Kelso and Suzy Newman
7-10 Actors

CAST OF CHARACTERS:

VALENTINE: Best buds with Proteus
PROTEUS: Best buds with Valentine and LOVES Julia
JULIA: LOVES Proteus
SILVIA: In love with Valentine
[1]**LUCETTA:** Julia's best friend!
[2]**ANTONIO (ANTONIA):** Proteus' father (mother)
[1]**DUKE (DUCHESS):** Silvia's father (mother)
SPEED: Valentine's lackey
LAUNCE: Proteus' lackey
[2]**CRAB:** Launce's dog (yes, a dog named Crab!)

The same actors can play the following part:
[1]LUCETTA and DUKE
[2]ANTONIO and CRAB

LUCETTA, SPEED, DUKE, and ANTONIO can all be played by one nimble actor with small costume piece changes.

ACT 1 SCENE 1

(enter VALENTINE and PROTEUS)

PROTEUS: Dude! DUDE! Valentine! Come on. Don't go! You're my best friend!

VALENTINE: Cease to persuade, Proteus! Knock it off! I want to see the wonders of the world abroad! I'm not going to be some dude who lives in his parents' basement and plays video games all day!

PROTEUS: I don't do that! Not all day.

VALENTINE: I know. Most of the time you're talking about Julia. Julia this *(big teasing sigh)*, Julia that *(sigh)*. I would ask you come with me, but I know you'd rather stay here in boring old Verona and think about Julia. Julia, Julia, Julia! *(kiss kiss kissy face to Proteus)*

PROTEUS: Fine! And someday you'll meet someone who you can't stop thinking about. And then you'll, think on thy Proteus! *(points to self)*

VALENTINE: Whatever. Take it easy.

(they secret handshake, fist bump, hug...)

VALENTINE: I'm out! *(exits)*

PROTEUS: *(calling after)* Later, dude! Have fun in Milan! *(pause)* Julia! *(sighs, exactly in the way Valentine mocked him; enter SPEED)*

SPEED: Proteus! Did you see my master?

PROTEUS: Hey, Speed! *(to audience)* Yeah, his name is Speed, don't ask, not like he's actually fast! Yeah, he left two seconds ago, to embark for Milan.

SPEED: Bummer! Twenty to one then he is shipp'd already.

(SPEED starts to go)

PROTEUS: Hey! Wait up! Did you give my note to Julia?

SPEED: Huh? Yeah, I gave it to her.

PROTEUS: What did she say? Did she ask about me?

SPEED: Truly, sir, I think you'll hardly win her.

PROTEUS: Why? How can you tell? What did she do?

SPEED: Like I said, she did nothing. You are meant for each other. *(exit SPEED)*

PROTEUS: Argggg!

(exit PROTEUS)

(enter JULIA and LUCETTA)

JULIA: OK, Lucetta, now that we're alone, let's talk about boys.

LUCETTA: Again?!

JULIA: Yes! Ok, what do you think of......Eglamour?

LUCETTA: Good dresser, nice hair, boring.

JULIA: What about.... Mercatio?

LUCETTA: Drives a nice car, can't speak in full sentences.

JULIA: What....about.....Proteus?

LUCETTA: WOW!!!

JULIA: He's pretty cute, right?

LUCETTA: SUPER cute.

JULIA: So... would you have me cast my love on him?

LUCETTA: Well, maybe you should peruse this paper.

JULIA: 'To Julia.' Who is it from?

LUCETTA: Valentine's page, and sent, I think, from Proteus.

JULIA: Hang on! You had a note for me this whole time?

LUCETTA: Don't be mad. Read it! Tell me what it says!

JULIA: Go, get you gone! I'll tear it to bits before I let you see what it says.

LUCETTA: No you won't.

JULIA: No? *(tears up the letter and throws the pieces into the air)*

LUCETTA: Rude!

(exit LUCETTA stomping her feet and pouting)

JULIA: *(gathering all the pieces of paper frantically)*

No, no, no, no, no, no! Look! Here's my name! 'kind Julia.' Here's his name...Proteus. And here's the word love. *(Resumes gathering the pieces)* Would've been easier if he'd sent a text!

(exit JULIA)

ACT 1 SCENE 3

(enter PROTEUS)

PROTEUS: Sweet love! Sweet lines! Sweet life! Oooo, poetic! I should write that down! *(to audience)* Look! She wrote me another note! She loves me, I love her. Life is perfect. Except we're afraid to tell our parents.

(enter ANTONIO)

ANTONIO: How now! what letter are you reading there?

PROTEUS: Oh! Hey dad! This letter? Oh, it's nothing.

ANTONIO: It's not nothing.

PROTEUS: Ahhhhh......It's a letter from Valentine, telling me what a great time he's having in Milan, yeah... that's what it says!

ANTONIO: Awesome! Glad to hear it! Because, you leave tomorrow to join Valentine in Milan.

PROTEUS: What!? Dad! No way! I don't want... I mean, I need some time. I've got some things to do.

ANTONIO: Like what?

PROTEUS: You know...things! Important things! And stuff! Lots of stuff!

ANTONIO: No more excuses! Go pack your bag.
(ANTONIO begins to exit)

PROTEUS: Fie!

ANTONIO: What was that?

PROTEUS: Fiiii......ne with me, Pops! *(ANTONIO exits)* I was afraid to show my father Julia's letter, lest he should take exceptions to my love; and my own lie of an excuse made it easier for him to send me away.

ANTONIO: *(Offstage)* Proteus! Get a move on!!

PROTEUS: Fie!!!

(exit PROTEUS)

ACT 2 SCENE 1

(enter VALENTINE and SPEED following)

VALENTINE: Ah, Silvia, Silvia! *(heavy sighs)*

SPEED: *(mocking)* Madam Silvia! Madam Silvia! Gag me.

VALENTINE: Knock it off! You don't know her.

SPEED: Do too. She's the one that you can't stop staring at. Makes me wanna barf.

VALENTINE: I do not stare!

SPEED: You do. AND you keep singing that silly love song. *(sing INSERT SAPPY LOVE SONG)* You used to be so much fun.

VALENTINE: Huh? *(heavy sigh, starts humming SAME LOVE SONG)*

SPEED: Never mind.

VALENTINE: I have loved her ever since I saw her. Here she comes!

SPEED: Great. *(to audience)* Watch him turn into a fool.

(enter SILVIA)

VALENTINE: Hey, Silvia.

SILVIA: Hey, Valentine. What's goin' on?

VALENTINE: Nothin'. What's goin' on with you?

SILVIA: Nothin'.

(pause)

VALENTINE: What are you doing later?

SILVIA: Not sure. Prob-ly nothin'. You?

VALENTINE: Me neither. Nothin'.

SILVIA: Yea?

VALENTINE: Probably.

SPEED: *(to audience)* Kill me now.

SILVIA: Well, I guess I better go.

VALENTINE: Oh, okay! See ya'..

(pause)

SILVIA: See ya' later maybe?

VALENTINE: Oh, yea! Maybe! Yea! Okay!

SILVIA: Bye.

VALENTINE: Bye!

(exit SILVIA)

SPEED: *(aside)* Wow. *(to VALENTINE)* Dude, what the heck was that?

VALENTINE: I think she has a boyfriend. I can tell.

SPEED: Dude! She is so into you! How could you not see that?

VALENTINE: Do you think?

SPEED: Come on. We'll talk it through over dinner. *(to audience)* Fool. Am I right?

(ALL exit)

ACT 2 SCENE 2

(enter PROTEUS and JULIA)

PROTEUS: Julia, please don't cry. When possibly I can, I will return.

JULIA: This is so unfair, *(sob)* we JUST found each other 10 minutes ago. Here! Take my ring to remember me.

PROTEUS: Awesome! And I'll give you mine.

(they exchange rings)

JULIA: And seal the bargain with a holy kiss. *(PROTEUS is excited)* But, not in front of my parents! *(points to audience)* Let's high-five!

PROTEUS: Julia, I promise you, I'll be thinking about you, like, aaallllllll the time! *(getting dramatic)* And I will love only you, Julia, forever and forever until the end of time.

JULIA: You promise?

PROTEUS: I promise! *("cross my heart and hope to die" motions)*

JULIA: I promise too!

(exit JULIA melodramatically sobbing)

PROTEUS: Julia, farewell! I am so so SO bummed. I LOVE HER SO MUCH!!!

(exit PROTEUS)

(enter LAUNCE, leading a dog and sobbing; he talks to the audience)

LAUNCE: Don't look at me. I can't stop crying. I have to leave my home to go with Proteus, because I work for him. Everyone in my family is devastated. Except my dog, Crab. He doesn't shed a tear. He just sits and scratches.

(CRAB looks at the audience, shrugs, scratches)

LAUNCE: See!? *(begins to cry again)*

(ALL exit)

(enter SILVIA, VALENTINE, and SPEED)

SILVIA: *(super flirty)* Hey, Vallie wallentine.

VALENTINE: *(same)* Hey, Princess Silvia wilvia.

SPEED: *(to audience)* Here we go again. *(breaking them up)* Look, here comes the Duke!

(enter DUKE)

DUKE: Hey, Valentine. There's another guy here, from Verona, who wants to work for me and I think you know him. His name is Proteus.

VALENTINE: Awesome! He's my best friend! This is great!

DUKE: Terrific, I'll send him out to say 'hi' before I put him to work.

(exit DUKE)

VALENTINE: This is my friend I told you about! The one who would have come along with me except that he is so in love and didn't want to leave his girlfriend.

SILVIA: Did they break up?

VALENTINE: Oh, no. He said many times he will love her till he dies. Kind of how I feel about a certain snooky-wooky, lovey pie...

SPEED: Kill me now!

(enter PROTEUS)

VALENTINE: Welcome, dear Proteus! Silvia, I want you to meet my best friend in the whole world. Proteus, meet Silvia.

SILVIA: *(shaking his hand)* Any friend of Valentine is a friend of mine.

PROTEUS: *(totally struck by her beauty, not letting go of her hand and acting delirious)* Bleen kack hoofta meep.

SILVIA: You're a crack up! We'll have a great time while you're here.

VALENTINE: No doubt. This is going to be the best.

PROTEUS: Plaaaff tooky ponga poop.

SILVIA: I'll leave you two to catch up.

(exit SILVIA)

VALENTINE: Proteus, fill me in! How does your lady? And how thrives your love?

PROTEUS: Oh, you don't want to hear about her. I know you don't like to talk about love.

VALENTINE: Well, that was before. I get it now! Because, guess what? I'm in love, too!

PROTEUS: With who?

VALENTINE: With Silvia!

PROTEUS: Her? But she loves you?

VALENTINE: Yes! And - don't tell anyone - we're going to run away and get married before her dad decides she has to marry some rich dude she doesn't even like and I can't believe I just blurted out all my plans to you!

PROTEUS: No worries. You know I always keep secrets. Those, and promises.

VALENTINE: And, dude, gotta go, I've been away from Silvia for like, two minutes, so... *(high-fives him)* later, bro!

(exit VALENTINE)

PROTEUS: *(Speaks to audience)* I am so so SO totally in love with Silvia! I know, I know... I said I was in love with... what'shername, but this time it's for real. Ooooo, this could be a problem. *(slowly)* My best friend is in love with the girl I love and the girl I used to love is in love with me and we exchanged promise rings and the girl I love now is in love with my best friend, who suddenly I don't really like that much - I don't know why. And they're eloping tonight! Ooooo I'm telling! *(pauses and looks back at audience)* Did you get all that? You have to love confusing Shakespeare comedy!

(exit PROTEUS)

(enter JULIA and LUCETTA)

JULIA: Lucetta! I have the best idea! But I need your help. I'm going to go to Milan and surprise Proteus!

LUCETTA: Wow! Are you sure that's a good idea?

JULIA: Yes! Now, help me make a disguise. I'm going to dress as a boy so no one will bother me.

LUCETTA: OK!

(ALL exit)

ACT 3 SCENE 1

(enter DUKE and PROTEUS)

DUKE: I heard you wanted to talk to me, Proteus. What's up?

PROTEUS: Ooooo, well....

DUKE: Spit it out.

PROTEUS: SilviareallylovesValentineandValentineloveheshandtonighttthey'regoingtoelope

DUKE: WHAT!?!? I am maaaaaaaad! Oh, looky, here comes Valentine. Make yourself scarce. *(exit PROTEUS; enter VALENTINE)*

DUKE: Say, Valentine, where are you going in such a hurry?

VALENTINE: Nowhere.

DUKE: Really? Because you're going in the direction of my daughter with a suspicious look in your eye.

VALENTINE: Whaaaa? Me? No.

DUKE: Seriously? Then why did I find a ladder outside her window with your name marked on it in Sharpie? Get out! You are banish-ed. Ba-nish-ed! And if I ever see you around here again, I'll..... I'll be really REALLY MAD!

(exit DUKE)

VALENTINE: And why not death rather than living torment? *(to audience)* Wow. I get really poetic when I'm miserable. *(pause)* Don't look at me anymore. I'm probably going to cry.

(enter PROTEUS, LAUNCE, and CRAB)

LAUNCE: *(CRAB points at Valentine)* Here he is!

PROTEUS: Valentine! We've been looking for you!

VALENTINE: Proteus, my best friend who would never betray me. You'll never guess what happened!

PROTEUS: I heard, I was listening from backstage. But don't worry, I'll help you!

VALENTINE: You will?! You are SUCH a good friend. How will you help me?

PROTEUS: You've got to go far away.

VALENTINE: Well, I'm not sure how that helps me, but I trust you, so OK.

(exit VALENTINE and PROTEUS)

LAUNCE: *(to audience)* I think my master is a kind of a knave. But I've got problems of my own. My dog just did something unmentionable on the palace rug. And so he wouldn't get in trouble, I told the Duke that I did it. *(to CRAB)* See how good I am to you? And all you've ever given me is fleas.

CRAB: *(to audience)* When you gotta go...you gotta go. Speaking of fleas... *(CRAB starts scratching; enter SPEED)*

SPEED: Launce! What's up?

LAUNCE: Your master got banished and my master told him to go far away.

SPEED: Then why are we still on stage?

LAUNCE: We're servants. We're here to be funny.

SPEED: Oh. Ok. Knock knock.

LAUNCE: Who's there.

SPEED: Hamlet.

LAUNCE: Hamlet who?

SPEED: Ham-let the dogs out! WOOF, WOOF WOOF WOOF WOOF!

(CRAB cracks up at this joke in a dog-like manner)

LAUNCE: *(exiting)* Terrible. I don't even know you.

SPEED: *(following)* Hey! That was pretty good! You try to do a Shakespearean knock knock joke. I don't think they even existed back then....

(ALL exit)

(enter JULIA in boys' clothes)

JULIA: Well, I'm here in Milan. Now to find Proteus. *(JULIA looks off-stage)* Here he comes. I'll surprise him. He'll love it!

(she hides; enter DUKE and PROTEUS)

PROTEUS: You have nothing to worry about. Valentine is gone and I'll go talk to Silvia and tell her that Valentine changed his mind about her. Trust me!

DUKE: Of course I trust you. Why wouldn't I?

(exit DUKE)

PROTEUS: *(to audience)* Yikes! I'm having a hard time keeping all of my lies straight!

JULIA: *(to audience)* There he is! He's going to be so happy to see me!

PROTEUS: *(to audience)* Here comes Silvia! *(to Silvia, in a mushy, dreamy voice)* Hiiiiii!

SILVIA: You again! Stop following me! You know I love Valentine.

PROTEUS: Just give me a chance!

SILVIA: No way! *(exiting)*

PROTEUS: Come on! I totally get you. Valentine doesn't get you the way I get you!

JULIA: Whoa. This is NOT going like I planned.

(PROTEUS sees her)

PROTEUS: You there, boy! What's your name?

JULIA: Um...uh, Sebastian? Yup, Sebastian, that's my name.

PROTEUS: You look familiar.... Anyway, I've got a job for you.

JULIA: Okay?

PROTEUS: See that girl that was just here? Go give her this ring that my girlfriend gave me that I said I'd keep forever. I'll pay you.

JULIA: Alas!

PROTEUS: What? What does that mean, and why did you say it?

JULIA: It's an interjection used as an exclamation to express pity or concern or grief. And I said it for your girlfriend.

PROTEUS: Boy, you're complicated.

JULIA: Because methinks that she loved you as well as you do love your lady Silvia, and now you're being really mean to her.

PROTEUS: Whatever. Give her the ring, then come tell me what she said.

(exit PROTEUS)

JULIA: Great. This is that LAST thing I want to do. *(enter SILVIA)* Are you Silvia?

SILVIA: What if I am?

JULIA: I was sent by Proteus to give you this ring.

SILVIA: No way. That's the ring his girlfriend, Julia, gave him and I'm not touching it. We girls have to stick together. Now excuse me while I run away into a dark and scary forest to find my boyfriend, Valentine. *(exit SILVIA)*

JULIA: *(to audience)* Wow. She's pretty cool.

(exit JULIA)

ACT 4 SCENE 1

(enter VALENTINE)

VALENTINE: Well, I'm still depressed but at least it's quiet and beautiful out here in the forest. *(Offstage ruckus)* Hark! Who comes here? *(hides to watch)*

(enter PROTEUS, SILVIA, and JULIA)

PROTEUS: Madam, this service I have done for you, I saved you from getting lost in this creepy forest.

VALENTINE: *(to audience)* How like a dream is this I see and hear! Love, lend me patience to forbear awhile. *(Valentine hides)*

SILVIA: O miserable, unhappy that I am!

PROTEUS: Nooooo! You WERE unhappy, but now I rescued you so now you ARE happy.

SILVIA: I would've rather been eaten by a lion, than have been rescued by you.

PROTEUS: You are really starting to frustrate me.

JULIA: *(to audience)* How do you think I feel?

SILVIA: Get this through your head, I don't like you! I will never go out with you!

PROTEUS: Oh, yes you will. *(goes in for the kiss; closes his eyes and puckers his lips toward her)*

SILVIA: *(running away, screaming)* Ewwwwww!

VALENTINE: *(jumping out)* Ruffian! You better back off if you know what's good for you!!!

PROTEUS/SILVIA/JULIA: Valentine!

VALENTINE: You are seriously the worst best friend ever!

PROTEUS: *(very over melodramatically)* My shame and guilt confounds me. Forgive me, Valentine. *(laying on the floor at his feet)*

VALENTINE: Well, OK. I forgive you. And you can go out with Silvia if you want.

SILVIA & JULIA: WHAT?!?!?!

SILVIA: Valentine! We need to talk!

PROTEUS: Sebastian! Where's that ring you were supposed to give Silvia?

JULIA: Here 'tis; this is it.

PROTEUS: Why, this is the ring I gave to Julia.

JULIA: Oops! Wrong one. THIS is the ring you sent to Silvia.

PROTEUS: How did you get that other one. That's the one I gave to Julia.

JULIA: Yes, it is. And guess what: Julia has brought it here.

(JULIA removes disguise; EVERYONE gasps)

PROTEUS: Uh, oh. How! Julia!

JULIA: Yes, it's me. The one who promised to be true to you. Boy, I feel like a real fool.

PROTEUS: No, please, don't. I'M the fool.

SILVIA: You got that right.

VALENTINE: How about we all just forget any of this ever happened and we have a double wedding!

PROTEUS: Yes! That's a great idea!

(enter DUKE and EVERYONE ELSE with general hubbub)

DUKE: What's happened? Is everyone OK? Where's my daughter?

VALENTINE: She's here. Safe and sound. I love her and she loves me and we'd like to get married.

DUKE: If this is what makes Silvia happy, I will consent to this marriage.

VALENTINE: I love happy endings! Come on everyone, let's go prepare for the weddings!

(ALL start rejoicing, except JULIA and SILVIA)

JULIA: HOLD IT! I know Shakespeare says I'm supposed to agree with this and we all live happily ever after, but... no way! I deserve better than someone who forgets me the second I'm out of sight.

SILVIA: You said it, sister!

JULIA: Proteus, here's your ring back. I'm going home.

(exit JULIA)

PROTEUS: *(exits chasing JULIA)* But, Julia, wait... let's talk about it!

SILVIA: Valentine, let's go plan our wedding!

(VALENTINE and SILVIA exit)

DUKE: Well this is awkward. Someone give me a script.

(script is handed to DUKE who looks through)

DUKE: Let's see... Here we go:

"Come, let us go, we will include all jars

With triumphs, mirth, and rare solemnity."

I'm not sure I understand all of that, but it's my line and it sounds like a happy ending to me. Let's go party!!!

(exit DUKE whooping it up)

The End

NOTES

The 25-Minute or so Two Gentlemen of Verona

By William Shakespeare
Creatively modified by
Brendan P. Kelso and Suzy Newman
10-16+ Actors

CAST OF CHARACTERS:

VALENTINE: Best buds with Proteus

PROTEUS: Best buds with Valentine and LOVES Julia

JULIA: LOVES Proteus

SILVIA: In love with Valentine

[1]**LUCETTA:** Julia's best friend!

[2]**ANTONIO (ANTONIA):** Proteus' father (mother)

[3]**PANTHINO:** Antonio's personal assistant

[4]**THURIO:** really likes Silvia

[1]**DUKE (DUCHESS):** Silvia's father (mother)

SPEED: Valentine's lackey

LAUNCE: Proteus' lackey

[3]**CRAB:** Launce's dog (yes, a dog named Crab!)

[1,2,3,4]**FOUR OUTLAWS:** outcasts from society living in the woods and wreaking havoc

The same actors can play the following part:

[1]LUCETTA, DUKE, and an OUTLAW

[2]ANTONIO and an OUTLAW

[3]PANTHINA, CRAB, and an OUTLAW

[4]THURIO and an OUTLAW

If Outlaws are doubled as actors, they do not come in the final scene

Extra outlaws can be added if needed

ACT 1 SCENE 1

(enter VALENTINE and PROTEUS)

PROTEUS: Dude! DUDE! Valentine! Come on. Don't go! You're my best friend!

VALENTINE: Cease to persuade, Proteus! Knock it off! I want to see the wonders of the world abroad! I'm not going to be some dude who lives in his parents' basement and plays video games all day!

PROTEUS: I don't do that! Not all day.

VALENTINE: I know. Most of the time you're talking about Julia. Julia this *(big teasing sigh)*, Julia that *(sigh)*. I would ask you come with me, but I know you'd rather stay here in boring old Verona and think about Julia. Julia, Julia, Julia! *(kiss kiss kissy face to Proteus)*

PROTEUS: Fine! And someday you'll meet someone who you can't stop thinking about. And then you'll, think on thy Proteus! *(points to self)*

VALENTINE: Whatever. Take it easy.

(they secret handshake, fist bump, hug...)

VALENTINE: I'm out! *(exits)*

PROTEUS: *(calling after)* Later, dude! Have fun in Milan! *(pause)* Julia! *(sighs, exactly in the way Valentine mocked him; enter SPEED)*

SPEED: Proteus! Did you see my master?

PROTEUS: Hey, Speed! *(to audience)* Yeah, his name is Speed, don't ask, not like he's actually fast! Yeah, he left two seconds ago, to embark for Milan.

SPEED: Bummer! Twenty to one then he is shipp'd already.

(SPEED starts to go)

PROTEUS: Hey! Wait up! Did you give my note to Julia?

SPEED: Huh? Yeah, I gave it to her.

PROTEUS: What did she say? Did she ask about me?

SPEED: Truly, sir, I think you'll hardly win her.

PROTEUS: Why? How can you tell? What did she do?

SPEED: Like I said, she did nothing. You are meant for each other. *(exit SPEED)*

PROTEUS: Argggg!

(exit PROTEUS)

(enter JULIA and LUCETTA)

JULIA: OK, Lucetta, now that we're alone, let's talk about boys.

LUCETTA: Again?!

JULIA: Yes! Ok, what do you think of......Eglamour?

LUCETTA: Good dresser, nice hair, boring.

JULIA: What about.... Mercatio?

LUCETTA: Drives a nice car, can't speak in full sentences.

JULIA: What....about.....Proteus?

LUCETTA: WOW!!!

JULIA: He's pretty cute, right?

LUCETTA: SUPER cute.

JULIA: So... would you have me cast my love on him?

LUCETTA: Well, maybe you should peruse this paper.

JULIA: 'To Julia.' Who is it from?

LUCETTA: Valentine's page, and sent, I think, from Proteus.

JULIA: Hang on! You had a note for me this whole time?

LUCETTA: Don't be mad. Read it! Tell me what it says!

JULIA: Go, get you gone! I'll tear it to bits before I let you see what it says.

LUCETTA: No you won't.

JULIA: No? *(tears up the letter and throws the pieces into the air)*

LUCETTA: Rude!

(exit LUCETTA stomping her feet and pouting)

JULIA: *(gathering all the pieces of paper frantically)*

No, no, no, no, no, no! Look! Here's my name! 'kind Julia.' Here's his name...Proteus. And here's the word love. *(Resumes gathering the pieces)* Would've been easier if he'd sent a text!

(exit JULIA)

ACT 1 SCENE 3

(enter ANTONIO and PANTHINO)

ANTONIO: Panthino, my friend, I'm going to send my son, Proteus, to Milan to hang out with his buddy, Valentine!

PANTHINO: I think that's a great idea. Look, here he comes!

(enter PROTEUS)

PROTEUS: *(enters not seeing PANTHINO and ANTONIO)* Sweet love! Sweet lines! Sweet life! Oooo, poetic! I should write that down! *(to audience)* Look! She wrote me another note! She loves me, I love her. Life is perfect. Except we're afraid to tell our parents.

ANTONIO: How now! what letter are you reading there?

PROTEUS: Oh! Hey, Dad! Nothing.

ANTONIO: It's not nothing.

PROTEUS: Ahhhhh......It's a letter from Valentine, telling me what a great time he's having in Milan, yeah... that's what it says!

ANTONIO: Awesome! Glad to hear it! Because, you leave tomorrow to join Valentine in Milan.

PROTEUS: What!? Dad! No way! I don't want... I mean, I need some time. I've got some things to do.

ANTONIO: Like what?

PROTEUS: You know...things! Important things! And stuff! Lots of stuff!

ANTONIO: No more excuses! Go pack your bag. *(ANTONIO and PANTHINO begin to exit)*

PROTEUS: Fie!

ANTONIO: What was that?

PROTEUS: Fiiii......ne with me, Pops! *(ANTONIO exits)* I was afraid to show my father Julia's letter, lest he should take exceptions to my love; and my own lie of an excuse made it easier for him to send me away.

ANTONIO: *(Offstage)* Proteus! Get a move on!!

PROTEUS: Fie!!!

(exit PROTEUS)

ACT 2 SCENE 1

(enter VALENTINE and SPEED following)

VALENTINE: Ah, Silvia, Silvia! *(heavy sighs)*

SPEED: *(mocking)* Madam Silvia! Madam Silvia! Gag me.

VALENTINE: Knock it off! You don't know her.

SPEED: Do too. She's the one that you can't stop staring at. Makes me wanna barf.

VALENTINE: I do not stare!

SPEED: You do. AND you keep singing that silly love song. *(sing INSERT SAPPY LOVE SONG)* You used to be so much fun.

VALENTINE: Huh? *(heavy sigh, starts humming SAME LOVE SONG)*

SPEED: Never mind.

VALENTINE: I have loved her ever since I saw her. Here she comes!

SPEED: Great. *(to audience)* Watch him turn into a fool.

(enter SILVIA)

VALENTINE: Hey, Silvia.

SILVIA: Hey, Valentine. What's goin' on?

VALENTINE: Nothin'. What's goin' on with you?

SILVIA: Nothin'.

(pause)

VALENTINE: What are you doing later?

SILVIA: Not sure. Prob-ly nothin'. You?

VALENTINE: Me neither. Nothin'.

SILVIA: Yea?

VALENTINE: Probably.

SPEED: *(to audience)* Kill me now.

SILVIA: Well, I guess I better go.

VALENTINE: Oh, okay! See ya'..

(pause)

SILVIA: See ya' later maybe?

VALENTINE: Oh, yea! Maybe! Yea! Okay!

SILVIA: Bye.

VALENTINE: Bye!

(exit SILVIA)

SPEED: *(aside)* Wow. *(to VALENTINE)* Dude, what the heck was that?

VALENTINE: I think she has a boyfriend. I can tell.

SPEED: Dude! She is so into you! How could you not see that?

VALENTINE: Do you think?

SPEED: Come on. We'll talk it through over dinner. *(to audience)* Fool. Am I right?

(ALL exit)

(enter PROTEUS and JULIA)

PROTEUS: Julia, please don't cry. When possibly I can, I will return.

JULIA: This is so unfair, *(sob)* we JUST found each other 10 minutes ago. Here! Take my ring to remember me.

PROTEUS: Awesome! And I'll give you mine.

(they exchange rings)

JULIA: And seal the bargain with a holy kiss. *(PROTEUS is excited)* But, not in front of my parents! *(points to audience)* Let's high-five!

PROTEUS: Julia, I promise you, I'll be thinking about you, like, aaallllllll the time! *(getting dramatic)* And I will love only you, Julia, forever and forever until the end of time.

JULIA: You promise?

PROTEUS: I promise! *("cross my heart and hope to die" motions)*

JULIA: I promise too!

(exit JULIA melodramatically sobbing)

PROTEUS: Julia, farewell!

(enter PANTHINO)

PANTHINO: Sir Proteus, you are stay'd for. Let's go!!

PROTEUS: Fine, I'm coming. I am so so SO bummed. I LOVE HER SO MUCH!!!

(both exit; enter LAUNCE, leading a dog and sobbing; he talks to the audience)

LAUNCE: Don't look at me. I can't stop crying. I have to leave my home to go with Proteus, because I work for him. Everyone in my family is devastated. Except my dog, Crab. He doesn't shed a tear. He just sits and scratches.

(CRAB looks at the audience, shrugs, scratches)

LAUNCE: See!? *(begins to cry again)*

(ALL exit)

(enter SILVIA, VALENTINE, THURIO, and SPEED; THURIO is off to side glaring at VALENTINE)

SILVIA: *(super flirty)* Hey, Vallie wallentine.

VALENTINE: *(same)* Hey, Princess Silvia wilvia.

SPEED: *(to Valentine)* Dude, that guy Thurio doesn't seem to like you.

VALENTINE: I know. He hates me, because Silvia's dad wants her to go out with him and Silvia likes me and not him but she lets him hang around so she doesn't disappoint her dad and she's not sure he'll approve of me. Get it?

SPEED: Wow, no.

VALENTINE: Ok, how about this; He likes her. She likes me. Her dad likes him, so he stays and hangs around. Now do you get it?

SPEED: Barely, Shakespeare sure likes confusing people in his comedies!

VALENTINE: A little bit, yea.

(exit SPEED)

VALENTINE: Hey Thurio, I don't like you.

THURIO: And I don't like you!

VALENTINE: What's that, Thurio? *(they draw swords)*

THURIO: You heard me!

VALENTINE: Want to fight!?

THURIO: Let's go!

SILVIA: A fine volley of words, gentlemen, but knock it off. Here comes my father, the Duke.

(enter DUKE)

DUKE: Hey, Valentine. There's another guy here, from Verona, who wants to work for me and I think you know him. His name is Proteus.

VALENTINE: Awesome! He's my best friend! This is great!

DUKE: Terrific, I'll send him out to say 'hi' before I put him to work.

(exit DUKE)

VALENTINE: This is my friend I told you about! The one who would have come along with me except that he is so in love and didn't want to leave his girlfriend.

SILVIA: Did they break up?

VALENTINE: Oh, no. He said many times he will love her till he dies. Kind of how I feel about...

THURIO: ACHEMMMM....

VALENTINE: Oh, that's right. You're still here.

SILVIA: Have done, have done; here comes the gentleman.

(enter PROTEUS)

VALENTINE: Welcome, dear Proteus! Silvia, I want you to meet my best friend in the whole world. Proteus, meet Silvia.

SILVIA: *(shaking his hand)* Any friend of Valentine is a friend of mine.

PROTEUS: *(totally struck by her beauty, not letting go of her hand and acting delirious)* Bleen kack hoofta meep.

SILVIA: You're a crack up! We'll have a great time while you're here.

VALENTINE: No doubt. This is going to be the best.

PROTEUS: Plaaaff tooky ponga poop.

THURIO: *(to audience)* Not another one. *(to SILVIA)* Madam, I think your father probably wants you and I to go see him for some reason.

SILVIA: Ok, fine. We'll leave you two to catch up. Come, Sir Thurio.

(exit SILVIA and THURIO)

VALENTINE: Proteus, fill me in! How does your lady? And how thrives your love?

PROTEUS: Oh, you don't want to hear about her. I know you don't like to talk about love.

VALENTINE: Well, that was before. I get it now! Because, guess what? I'm in love, too!

PROTEUS: With who?

VALENTINE: With Silvia!

PROTEUS: Her? But she loves you?

VALENTINE: Yes! And - don't tell anyone - we're going to run away and get married before her dad decides she has to marry Thurio and I can't believe I just blurted out all my plans to you!

PROTEUS: No worries. You know I always keep secrets. Those, and promises.

VALENTINE: And, dude, gotta go, I've been away from Silvia for like, two minutes, so... *(high-fives him)* later, bro!

(exit VALENTINE)

PROTEUS: *(speaks to audience)* I am so so SO totally in love with Silvia! I know, I know... I said I was in love with... what'shername, but this time it's for real. Ooooo, this could be a problem. *(slowly)* My best friend is in love with the girl I love and the girl I used to love is in love with me and we exchanged promise rings and the girl I love now is in love with my best friend, who suddenly I don't really like that much - I don't know why. And they're eloping tonight! Ooooo I'm telling! *(pauses and looks back at audience)* Did you get all that? You have to love confusing Shakespeare comedy!

(exit PROTEUS)

(enter JULIA and LUCETTA)

JULIA: Lucetta! I have the best idea! But I need your help. I'm going to go to Milan and surprise Proteus!

LUCETTA: Wow! Are you sure that's a good idea?

JULIA: Yes! Now, help me make a disguise. I'm going to dress as a boy so no one will bother me.

LUCETTA: OK!

(ALL exit)

ACT 3 SCENE 1

(enter DUKE, THURIO, and PROTEUS)

DUKE: I heard you wanted to talk to me, Proteus. What's up?

PROTEUS: Ooooo, well....

DUKE: Spit it out.

PROTEUS: SilviahatesThurioandlovesValentineand-tonightthey'regoingtoelope!

DUKE: WHAT!?!? I am maaaaaaaad! Oh, looky, here comes Valentine. Make yourself scarce. *(exit PROTEUS; enter VALENTINE)*

DUKE: Say, Valentine, where are you going in such a hurry?

VALENTINE: Nowhere.

DUKE: Really? Because you're going in the direction of my daughter with a suspicious look in your eye.

VALENTINE: Whaaaa? Me? No.

DUKE: Seriously? Then why did I find a ladder outside her window with your name marked on it in Sharpie? Get out! You are banish-ed. Ba-nish-ed! And if I ever see you around here again, I'll..... I'll be really REALLY MAD!

(exit DUKE)

VALENTINE: And why not death rather than living torment? *(to audience)* Wow. I get really poetic when I'm miserable. *(pause)* Don't look at me anymore. I'm probably going to cry.

(enter PROTEUS, LAUNCE, and CRAB)

LAUNCE: Here he is!

(CRAB points at Valentine)

PROTEUS: Valentine! We've been looking for you!

VALENTINE: Proteus, my best friend who would never betray me. You'll never guess what happened!

PROTEUS: I heard, I was listening from backstage. But don't worry, I'll help you!

VALENTINE: You will?! You are SUCH a good friend. How will you help me?

PROTEUS: You've got to go far away.

VALENTINE: Well, I'm not sure how that helps me, but I trust you, so OK.

(exit VALENTINE and PROTEUS)

LAUNCE: *(to audience)* I think my master is a kind of a knave. But I've got problems of my own. My dog just did something unmentionable on the palace rug. And so he wouldn't get in trouble, I told the Duke that I did it. *(to CRAB)* See how good I am to you? And all you've ever given me is fleas.

CRAB: *(to audience)* When you gotta go...you gotta go. Speaking of fleas... *(CRAB starts scratching; enter SPEED)*

SPEED: Launce! What's up?

LAUNCE: Your master got banished and my master told him to go far away.

SPEED: Then why are we still on stage?

LAUNCE: We're servants. We're here to be funny.

SPEED: Oh. Ok. Knock knock.

LAUNCE: Who's there.

SPEED: Hamlet.

LAUNCE: Hamlet who?

SPEED: Ham-let the dogs out! WOOF, WOOF WOOF WOOF WOOF!

(CRAB cracks up at this joke in a dog-like manner)

LAUNCE: *(exiting)* Terrible. I don't even know you.

SPEED: *(following)* Hey! That was pretty good! You try to do a Shakespearean knock knock joke. I don't think they even existed back then....

(ALL exit)

(enter JULIA in boys' clothes)

JULIA: Well, I'm here in Milan. Now to find Proteus. *(JULIA looks off-stage)* Here he comes. I'll surprise him. He'll love it!

(she hides; enter DUKE, THURIO and PROTEUS)

PROTEUS: You have nothing to worry about. Valentine is gone and I'll go talk to Silvia and tell her Thurio is the guy for her. Trust me!

DUKE: Oh, we trust you. Don't we, Thurio?

THURIO: Why wouldn't we?

(exit DUKE and THURIO)

PROTEUS: *(to audience)* Yikes! I'm having a hard time keeping all of my lies straight!

JULIA: *(to audience)* There he is! He's going to be so happy to see me!

PROTEUS: *(to audience)* Here comes Silvia! *(to Silvia, in a mushy, dreamy voice)* Hiiiiii!

SILVIA: You again! Stop following me! You know I love Valentine.

PROTEUS: Just give me a chance!

SILVIA: No way! *(exiting)*

PROTEUS: Come on! I totally get you. Valentine doesn't get you the way I get you!

JULIA: Whoa. This is NOT going like I planned.

(PROTEUS sees her)

PROTEUS: You there, boy! What's your name?

JULIA: Um...uh, Sebastian? Yup, Sebastian, that's my name.

PROTEUS: You look familiar.... Anyway, I've got a job for you.

JULIA: Okay?

PROTEUS: See that girl that was just here? Go give her this ring that my girlfriend gave me that I said I'd keep forever. I'll pay you.

JULIA: Alas!

PROTEUS: What? What does that mean, and why did you say it?

JULIA: It's an interjection used as an exclamation to express pity or concern or grief. And I said it for your girlfriend.

PROTEUS: Boy, you're complicated.

JULIA: Because methinks that she loved you as well as you do love your lady Silvia, and now you're being really mean to her.

PROTEUS: Whatever. Give her the ring, then come tell me what she said.

(exit PROTEUS)

JULIA: Great. This is that LAST thing I want to do. *(enter SILVIA)* Are you Silvia?

SILVIA: What if I am?

JULIA: I was sent by Proteus to give you this ring.

SILVIA: No way. That's the ring his girlfriend, Julia, gave him and I'm not touching it. We girls have to stick together. Now excuse me while I run away into a dark and scary forest to find my boyfriend, Valentine. *(exit SILVIA)*

JULIA: *(to audience)* Wow. She's pretty cool.

(exit JULIA)

ACT 4 SCENE 1

(enter OUTLAWS with SILVIA)

FIRST OUTLAW: Come, come, be patient; we must bring you to our captain.

SILVIA: HELP!!! Stranger danger!!

SECOND OUTLAW: Make her stop!

THIRD OUTLAW: No, don't hurt her. We're called outlaws, but we never really do anything bad.

FOURTH OUTLAW: Did you hear that, lady? We won't hurt you.

SILVIA: O Valentine, this I endure for thee!

SECOND OUTLAW: Did she say Valentine?

THIRD OUTLAW: She did. That's the same name as the guy we found wandering in the forest, crying.

FOURTH OUTLAW: The one who joined our gang as our leader.

FIRST OUTLAW: Shakespeare is so full of coincidences!

(ALL exit)

ACT 5 SCENE 1

(enter VALENTINE)

VALENTINE: Well, I'm still depressed but at least it's quiet and beautiful out here in the forest. *(Offstage ruckus)* Hark! Who comes here? *(hides to watch)*

(enter PROTEUS, SILVIA, and JULIA)

PROTEUS: Madam, this service I have done for you, I saved you from those..... whatever they were.

VALENTINE: *(to audience)* How like a dream is this I see and hear! Love, lend me patience to forbear awhile. *(Valentine hides)*

SILVIA: O miserable, unhappy that I am!

PROTEUS: Nooooo! You WERE unhappy, but now I rescued you so now you ARE happy.

SILVIA: I would've rather been eaten by a lion, than have been rescued by you.

PROTEUS: You are really starting to frustrate me.

JULIA: *(to audience)* How do you think I feel?

SILVIA: Get this through your head, I don't like you! I will never go out with you!

PROTEUS: Oh, yes you will. *(goes in for the kiss; closes his eyes and puckers his lips toward her)*

SILVIA: *(running away, screaming)* Ewwwwww!

VALENTINE: *(jumping out)* Ruffian! You better back off if you know what's good for you!!!

PROTEUS/SILVIA/JULIA: Valentine!

VALENTINE: You are seriously the worst best friend ever!

PROTEUS: *(very over melodramatically)* My shame and guilt confounds me. Forgive me, Valentine. *(laying on the floor at his feet)*

VALENTINE: Well, OK. I forgive you. And you can go out with Silvia if you want.

SILVIA & JULIA: WHAT?!?!?!

SILVIA: Valentine! We need to talk!

PROTEUS: Sebastian! Where's that ring you were supposed to give Silvia?

JULIA: Here 'tis; this is it.

PROTEUS: Why, this is the ring I gave to Julia.

JULIA: Oops! Wrong one. THIS is the ring you sent to Silvia.

PROTEUS: How did you get that other one. That's the one I gave to Julia.

JULIA: Yes, it is. And guess what: Julia has brought it here.

(JULIA removes disguise; EVERYONE gasps)

PROTEUS: Uh, oh. How! Julia!

JULIA: Yes, it's me. The one who promised to be true to you. Boy, I feel like a real fool.

PROTEUS: No, please, don't. I'M the fool.

SILVIA: You got that right.

VALENTINE: How about we all just forget any of this ever happened and we have a double wedding!

PROTEUS: Yes! That's a great idea!

(enter DUKE and THURIO and EVERYONE ELSE with general hubbub; LAUNCE and SPEED go to greet their respective masters; CRAB goes up to PROTEUS and growls)

DUKE: What's happened? Is everyone OK? Where's my daughter?

VALENTINE: She's here. Safe and sound. I saved her and we'd like to get married.

THURIO: No way. She's mine.

VALENTINE: *(pulls sword)* Thurio, back off! Let's not make this comedy a tragedy! I've saved her and she loves me.

DUKE: Thurio, he's right. My daughter loves him and I will consent to their marriage.

THURIO: Well, this stinks!

VALENTINE: I love happy endings! Come on everyone, let's go prepare for the weddings!

(ALL start rejoicing, except JULIA and SILVIA)

JULIA: HOLD IT! I know Shakespeare says I'm supposed to agree with this and we all live happily ever after, but... no way! I deserve better than someone who forgets me the second I'm out of sight.

SILVIA: You said it, sister!

JULIA: Proteus, here's your ring back. I'm going home.

(exit JULIA)

PROTEUS: *(exits chasing JULIA)* But, Julia, wait... let's talk about it!

SILVIA: Valentine, let's go plan our wedding!

(VALENTINE and SILVIA exit)

DUKE: Well this is awkward. Someone give me a script.

(script is handed to DUKE who looks through)

DUKE: Let's see... Here we go:

"Come, let us go, we will include all jars

With triumphs, mirth, and rare solemnity."

I'm not sure I understand all of that, but it's my line and it sounds like a happy ending to me. Let's go party!!!

(exit DUKE whooping it up)

The End

Sneak Peeks at other Playing With Plays books:

King Lear for Kids

ACT 1 SCENE 1

KING LEAR's palace

(enter FOOL entertaining the audience with jokes, dancing, juggling, Hula Hooping... whatever the actor's skill may be; enter KENT)

KENT: Hey, Fool!

FOOL: What did you call me?!

KENT: I called you Fool.

FOOL: That's my name, don't wear it out! *(to audience)* Seriously, that's my name in the play!

(enter LEAR, CORNWALL, ALBANY, GONERIL, REGAN, and CORDELIA)

LEAR: The lords of France and Burgundy are outside. They both want to marry you, Cordelia.

ALL: Ooooooo!

LEAR: *(to audience)* Between you and me she IS my favorite child! *(to the girls)* Daughters, I need to talk to you about something. It's a really big deal.

GONERIL & REGAN: Did you buy us presents?

LEAR: This is even better than presents!

GONERIL & REGAN: Goody, goody!!!

CORDELIA: Father, your love is enough for me.

LEAR: Give me the map there, Kent. Girls, I'm tired. I've made a decision: Know that we - and by 'we' I mean 'me' - have divided in three our kingdom...

KENT: Whoa! Sir, dividing the kingdom may cause chaos! People could die!

FOOL: Well, this IS a tragedy...

LEAR: You worry too much, Kent. I'm giving it to my daughters so their husbands can be rich and powerful... like me!

CORNWALL & ALBANY: Sweet!

GONERIL & REGAN: Wait... what?

CORDELIA: This is olden times. That means that everything we own belongs to our husbands.

GONERIL & REGAN: Olden times stink!

CORDELIA: Truth.

LEAR: So, my daughters, tell your daddy how much you love him. Goneril, our eldest-born, speak first.

GONERIL: Sir, I love you more than words can say! More than outer space, puppies and cotton candy! I love you more than any child has ever loved a father in the history of the entire world, dearest Pops!

CORDELIA: *(to audience)* Holy moly! Surely, he won't be fooled by that. *(to self)* Love, and be silent.

LEAR: Thanks, sweetie! I'm giving you this big chunk of the kingdom here. What says our second daughter, Our dearest Regan, wife to Cornwall? Speak.

REGAN: What she said, Daddy... times a thousand!

CORDELIA: *(to audience)* What?! I love my father more than either of them. But I can't express it in words. My love's more richer than my tongue.

LEAR: Wow, Regan! You get this big hunk of the kingdom. Cordelia, what can you tell me to get this giant piece of kingdom as your own? Speak.

CORDELIA: Nothing, my lord.

LEAR: Nothing?!?

CORDELIA: Nothing.

LEAR: Come on, now. Nothing will come of nothing.

CORDELIA: I love you as a daughter loves her father.

LEAR: Try a little, harder, sweetie!

CORDELIA: Why are my sisters married if they give you all their love?

LEAR: How did you get so mean?

CORDELIA: Father, I will not insult you by telling you my love is like... as big as a whale.

LEAR: *(getting mad)* Fine. I'll split your share between your sisters.

REGAN, GONERIL, & CORNWALL: Yessss!

KENT: Whoa! Let's all just calm down a minute!

LEAR: Peace, Kent! You don't want to mess with me right now. I told you she was my favorite...

GONERIL & REGAN: What!?

LEAR: ...and she can't even tell me she loves me more than a whale? Nope. Now I'm mad.

KENT: Royal Lear, really...

LEAR: Kent, I'm pretty emotional right now! You better not try to talk me out of this...

KENT: Sir, you're acting ... insane.

Sneak peek of
The Three Musketeers
for Kids

(ATHOS and D'ARTAGNAN enter)

ATHOS: Glad you could make it. I have engaged two of my friends as seconds.

D'ARTAGNAN: Seconds?

ATHOS: Yeah, they make sure we fight fair. Oh, here they are now!

(enter ARAMIS and PORTHOS singing, "Bad boys, bad boys, watcha gonna do...")

PORTHOS: Hey! I'm fighting him in an hour. I am going to fight... because...well... I am going to fight!

ARAMIS: And I fight him at two o'clock! Ours is a theological quarrel. *(does a thinking pose)*

D'ARTAGNAN: Yeah, yeah, yeah... I'll get to you soon!

ATHOS: We are the Three Musketeers; Athos, Porthos, and Aramis.

D'ARTAGNAN: Whatever, Ethos, Pathos, and Logos, let's just finish this! *(swords crossed and are about to fight; enter JUSSAC and cardinal's guards)*

PORTHOS: The cardinal's guards! Sheathe your swords, gentlemen.

JUSSAC: Dueling is illegal! You are under arrest!

ARAMIS: *(to ATHOS and PORTHOS)* There are five of them and we are but three.

D'ARTAGNAN: *(steps forward to join them)* It appears to me we are four! I have the spirit; my heart is that of a Musketeer.

PORTHOS: Great! I love fighting!

(Musketeers say "Fight, fight fight!...Fight, fight, fight!" as they are fighting; D'ARTAGNAN fights JUSSAC and it's the big fight; JUSSAC is wounded and exits; the 3 MUSKETEERS cheer)

ATHOS: Well done! Let's go see Treville and the king!

ARAMIS: And we don't have to kill you now!

PORTHOS: And let's get some food, too! I'm hungry!

D'ARTAGNAN: *(to audience)* This is fun!

(ALL exit)

ACT 2 SCENE 1

(enter 3 MUSKETEERS, D'ARTAGNAN, and TREVILLE)

TREVILLE: The king wants to see you, and he's not too happy you killed a few of the cardinal's guards.

(enter KING)

KING: *(yelling)* YOU GUYS HUMILIATED THE CARDINAL'S GUARDS!

ATHOS: Sire, they attacked us!

KING: Oh...Well then, bravo! I hear D'Artagnan beat the cardinal's best swordsman! Brave young man! Here's some money for you. Enjoy! *(hands money to D'ARTAGNAN)*

D'ARTAGNAN: Sweet!

(ALL exit)

Oliver Twist
for Kids

(enter FAGIN, SIKES, DODGER and NANCY)

DODGER: So that Oliver kid got caught by the police.

FAGIN: He could tell them all our secrets and get us in trouble; we've got to find him. Like, in the next 30 seconds or so.

SIKES: Send Nancy. She's good at getting information quick.

NANCY: Nope. Don't wanna go, Sikes. I like the kid.

SIKES: She'll go, Fagin.

NANCY: No, she won't, Fagin.

SIKES: Yes, she will, Fagin.

NANCY: Fine! Grrrrr....

(NANCY sticks out her tongue at SIKES and storms offstage, then immediately returns)

NANCY: Okay, I checked with my sources and, some gentleman took him home to take care of him.

(NANCY, DODGER and SIKES stare at FAGIN waiting for direction)

FAGIN: Where?

NANCY: I don't know.

FAGIN: WHAT!?!? *(waiting)* Well don't just stand there, GO FIND HIM! *(to audience)* Can't find any good help these days!

(ALL run offstage, bumping into each other in their haste)

ACT 2 SCENE 2

(enter OLIVER)

OLIVER: *(to audience)* I'm out running an errand for Mr. Brownlow to prove that I'm a trustworthy boy. I can't keep hanging out with thieves, right?

(enter NANCY, who runs over to OLIVER and grabs him; SIKES, FAGIN, and DODGER enter shortly after and follow NANCY)

NANCY: Oh my dear brother! I've found him! Oh! Oliver! Oliver!

OLIVER: What!?!? I don't have a sister!

NANCY: You do now, kid. Let's go. *(she drags OLIVER to FAGIN)*

FAGIN: Dodger, take Oliver and lock him up.

DODGER: *(to OLIVER)* Sorry, dude. *(DODGER and OLIVER start to exit)*

OLIVER: Aw, man! Seriously? I just found a good home...

NANCY: Don't be too mean to him, Fagin.

OLIVER: *(as he's exiting)* Yeah, don't be too mean to me, Fagin!

SIKES: *(mimicking NANCY)* Don't be mean, Fagin. Wah, wah, wah. Look, I need Oliver to help me rob a house, okay? He is just the size I want to fit through the window. All sneaky ninja like.

The Tempest for Kids

PROSPERO: Hast thou, spirit, performed to point the tempest that I bade thee?

ARIEL: What? Was that English?

PROSPERO: *(Frustrated)* Did you make the storm hit the ship?

ARIEL: Why didn't you say that in the first place? Oh yeah! I rocked that ship! They didn't know what hit them.

PROSPERO: Why, that's my spirit! But are they, Ariel, safe?

ARIEL: Not a hair perished.

PROSPERO: Woo-hoo! All right. We've got more work to do.

ARIEL: Wait a minute. You're still going to free me, right, Master?

PROSPERO: Oh, I see. Is it sooooo terrible working for me? Huh? Remember when I saved you from that witch? Do you? Remember when that blue-eyed hag locked you up and left you for dead? Who saved you? Me, that's who!

ARIEL: I thank thee, master.

PROSPERO: I will free you in two days, okay? Sheesh. Patience is a virtue, or haven't you heard. Right. Where was I? Oh yeah... I need you to disguise yourself like a sea nymph and then... *(PROSPERO whispers something in ARIEL'S ear)* Got it?

ARIEL: Got it. *(ARIEL exits)*

PROSPERO: *(to MIRANDA)* Awake, dear heart, awake!

(MIRANDA yawns loudly)

PROSPERO: Shake it off. Come on. We'll visit Caliban, my slave.

MIRANDA: The witch's son? You mean the MONSTER! He's creepy and stinky!!!

PROSPERO: Mysterious and sneaky,

MIRANDA: Altogether freaky,

MIRANDA & PROSPERO: He's Caliban the slave!!! *(snap, snap!)*

PROSPERO: *(Calls offstage)* What, ho! Slave! Caliban!

(enter CALIBAN)

CALIBAN: Oh, look it's the island stealers! This is my home! My mother, the witch, left it to me and now you treat me like dirt.

MIRANDA: Oh boo-hoo! I used to feel sorry for you, I even taught you our language, but you tried to hurt me so now we have to lock you in that cave.

CALIBAN: I wish I had never learned your language!

PROSPERO: Go get us wood! If you don't, I'll rack thee with old cramps, and fill all thy bones with aches!

CALIBAN: *(to AUDIENCE)* He's so mean to me! But I have to do what he says. ANNOYING! *(exit CALIBAN)*

(enter FERDINAND led by "invisible" ARIEL)

ARIEL: *(Singing)* Who let the dogs out?! Woof, woof, woof!! *(Spookily)* The watchdogs bark; bow-wow, bow-wow!

FERDINAND: *(Dancing across stage)* Where should this music be? Where is it taking me! What's going on?

Frankenstein for Kids

ACT 1 SCENE 1

(enter WALDMAN and VICTOR)

WALDMAN: Victor! Come in! You look so tired. Do you need me to give you a hand?

VICTOR: Ahhh.... No. I'm fine, Professor Waldman! I've been working on an experiment. There's just so much to be done.

WALDMAN: You remind me of myself as a young student! So few of us are willing to give our right arms for science!

VICTOR: *(to audience)* You have no idea! I will solve the mysteries of creation! *(laughs madly)*

WALDMAN: Pardon me?

VICTOR: I said...ahhh... I have a good idea! I must get back to work. Excuse me! *(VICTOR exits)*

WALDMAN: I can't wait to hear all about it! I have no doubt of your success! Bye! *(to audience)* Strange kid.

(WALDMAN exits; VICTOR pops back on stage and addresses audience)

VICTOR: I want to tell him, but he'd think I'm mad! You see, I've figured out how to make dead things live again! *(laughs madly, exits and returns with arms and legs)* I've been through dozens of graves and hospitals. Finally, I have everything I need!

(exits, laughing madly)

(VICTOR enters dragging MONSTER who is laying under a sheet)

VICTOR: *(to audience)* I see by your eagerness that you expect to see how it's done. Ha! If I showed you, you'd be...SHOCKED! Time to become the world's first bodybuilder! *(VICTOR laughs madly as he raises the sheet to hide himself and MONSTER)* To bolt or not to bolt, THAT is the question! *(there's a clap of thunder, then VICTOR yanks away sheet)*

MONSTER: *(sits up in monster voice)* GRR!!! GRR!!!

VICTOR: It's alive! It's alive!! IT'S ALIVE!!!

MONSTER: You never said that in the book!

VICTOR: I know but, it's more fun to say...IT'S ALIVE!

MONSTER: *(MONSTER takes one step towards VICTOR)* GRR!!!

VICTOR: OK!!! AAGH!!! Monster! *(screams and runs to other side of stage and hides under the sheet)*

MONSTER: *(lifts sheet)* Now THAT'S what you said in the book! UGH!!!

(VICTOR runs away screaming, MONSTER takes the sheet and wears it like a cloak, exits)

The Jungle Book for Kids

PARENT WOLF: Oh hi, Bagheera. What's happening in the life of a panther?

BAGHEERA: I wanted to warn you. Shere Khan's in town again.

PARENT WOLF: The tiger? What's he doing in this part of the jungle?

BAGHEERA: What tigers do. You know, hunt, eat, hunt again, eat... hunt...eat... *(trailing off)*

PARENT WOLF: *(play-acting like a tiger)* Oh look at me, I'm a mean ol' tiger, roar!!! *(there is a LOUD ROAR and GROWL from offstage, PARENT WOLF is a bit shocked)*

BAGHEERA: Listen! That's him now!

(enter MOWGLI, running off-balance, and falling down)

PARENT WOLF: Whoa! A man's cub! Look! *(ALL turn to look at MOWGLI)* How little and so... smelly, but cute! *(starts petting his hair)*

(BAGHEERA sneaks over to MOWGLI and whispers something in his ear. MOWGLI sighs and gets down on his knees to appear smaller; he remains on his knees throughout the rest of the scene and ACT1 SCENE 2)

MOWGLI: *(very sarcastically)* Gaa gaa. Goo goo.

(SHERE KHAN enters. PARENT WOLF hides MOWGLI behind her back)

SHERE KHAN: A man's cub went this way. Its parents have run off. Give it to me. I'll uh... take care of him... *(as he rubs his belly)* you can TOTALLY trust me! *(gives* *the audience a big evil smile)*

PARENT WOLF: You are NOT the boss of us.

SHERE KHAN: Excuse me?! Do you know who I am? It is I, Shere Khan, who speaks! I'm kind of a big deal. And scary! GRRRRR.

PARENT WOLF: The man's cub is mine; he shall not be killed! So beat it; you don't scare us.

SHERE KHAN: Fine. But I'll get him some day, make no mistake! Muahahahahaha! ROAR! *(SHERE KHAN exits)*

PARENT WOLF: *(to MOWGLI)* Mowgli the Frog I will call thee. Lie still, little frog.

MOWGLI: *(to PARENT WOLF)* Frog?

PARENT WOLF: *(to MOWGLI and audience)* Yeah, I guess Rudyard Kipling liked frogs! But now we have to see what the wolf leader says.

(enter AKELA, BAGHEERA, and BALOO)

AKELA: Okay, wolves, let's get this meeting started! Howl!

WOLVES: Howl!! *(ALL WOLVES howl)*

PARENT WOLF: Akela, our great leader, I'd like to present the newest member of our pack, Mowgli the Frog!

AKELA: Hmmm, Frog, huh? If you say so.

(enter SHERE KHAN)

SHERE KHAN: ROAR! The cub is mine! Give him to me!

AKELA: Who speaks for this cub?

BALOO: *(speaking in a big, deep bear voice!)* I, Baloo the Bear, I speak for the man's cub. I myself will teach him the ways of the jungle.

Sneak peek of
Christmas Carol
for Kids

(enter GHOST PRESENT wearing a robe and holding a turkey leg and a goblet)

GHOST PRESENT: Wake up, Scrooge! I am the Ghost of Christmas Present. Look upon me!

SCROOGE: I'm looking. Not that impressed. But let's get on with it.

GHOST PRESENT: Touch my robe! *(SCROOGE touches GHOST PRESENT's robe. Pause. They look at each other)* Er...it must be broken. Guess we walk. Come on. *(they begin walking downstage)*

SCROOGE: Where are we going?

GHOST PRESENT: Your employee, Bob Cratchit's house. Oh look, here we are.

(enter BOB, MRS. CRATCHIT, MARTHA CRATCHIT, and TINY TIM, who has a crutch in one hand; they are all holding bowls)

BOB: *(to audience)* Hi, we're the Cratchit family. We are a REALLY happy family!

MRS. CRATCHIT: *(to audience)* Yes, but we're REALLY poor, too. Thanks to HIS boss! *(pointing at BOB)*

MARTHA: *(to audience)* Yeah, as you can see our bowls are empty. *(shows empty bowl)* We practically survive off air.

TINY TIM: *(to audience)* But we're happy!

MRS. CRATCHIT: *(to audience; overly sappy)* Because we have each other.

TINY TIM: And love!

SCROOGE: *(to GHOST PRESENT)* Seriously, are they for real?

GHOST PRESENT: Yep! Adorable, isn't it?

BOB: A merry Christmas to us all.

TINY TIM: God bless us every one!

SCROOGE: Spirit, tell me if Tiny Tim will live.

GHOST PRESENT: *(puts hands to head as if looking into the future)* Ooooo, not so good...I see a vacant seat in the poor chimney corner, and a crutch without an owner. If SOMEBODY doesn't change SOMETHING, the child will die.

SCROOGE: No, no! Say he will be spared.

GHOST PRESENT: Nope, can't do that, sorry. Unless SOMEONE decides to change... hint, hint.

BOB: A Christmas toast to my boss, Mr. Scrooge! The founder of the feast!

MRS. CRATCHIT: *(angrily)* Oh sure, Mr. Scrooge! If he were here I'd give him a piece of my mind to feast upon. What an odious, stingy, hard, unfeeling man!

BOB: Dear, it's Christmas day. He's not THAT bad. *(Pause)* He's just... THAT sad. *(BOB holds up his bowl)* Come on, kids, to Scrooge! He probably needs it more than us!

MARTHA & TINY TIM: *(holding up their bowls)* To Scrooge!

MRS. CRATCHIT: *(muttering)* Thanks for nothing.

BOB: That's not nice.

MARTHA: And we Cratchits are ALWAYS nice. Read the book, Mom.

MRS. CRATCHIT: Sorry.

(the CRATCHIT FAMILY exits)

SCROOGE: She called me odious! Do I really smell that bad?

GHOST PRESENT: Odious doesn't mean you stink. Although in this case you do... According to the dictionary, odious means "unequivocally detestable." I mean, you are a toad sometimes Mr. Scrooge.

SCROOGE: Wow... that's kind of... mean.

ABOUT THE AUTHORS

SUZY NEWMAN, is an actor and theatre director based in San Luis Obispo, CA. Her affinity for theatre surfaced later than most and after graduating from college, she jumped ship from her childhood career path and planted her feet firmly on the stage. Shakespeare dominated her first decade of acting and she's played many of his great women - and a few of his men. She earned her MFA in Acting in 2000 and continues to freelance as an actor, director, acting coach, teacher and writer. She is also the singer for a rock band, which is simply another opportunity to laugh and create with a group of like-minded people.

BRENDAN P. KELSO came to writing modified Shakespeare scripts when he was taking time off from work to be at home with his newly born son. "It just grew from there". Within months, he was being asked to offer classes in various locations and acting organizations along the Central Coast of California. Originally employed as an engineer, Brendan never thought about writing. However, his unique personality, humor, and love for engaging the kids with The Bard has led him to leave the engineering world and pursue writing as a new adventure in life! He has always believed, "the best way to learn is to have fun!" Brendan makes his home on the Central Coast of California and loves to spend time with his wife and son.

CAST AUTOGRAPHS

Made in the USA
Columbia, SC
29 November 2021

50010202R00057